W9-CLW-669

STINKY

MARY RILEY STYLES PUBLIC LIBRARY
120 NORTH VIRGINIA AVENUE
FALLS CHURCH, VA 22046
(703) 248-5030

A TOON BOOK BY

ELEANOR DAVIS

TOON BOOKS, A DIVISION OF RAW JUNIOR, LLC, NEW YORK

WWW.TOON-BOOKS.COM

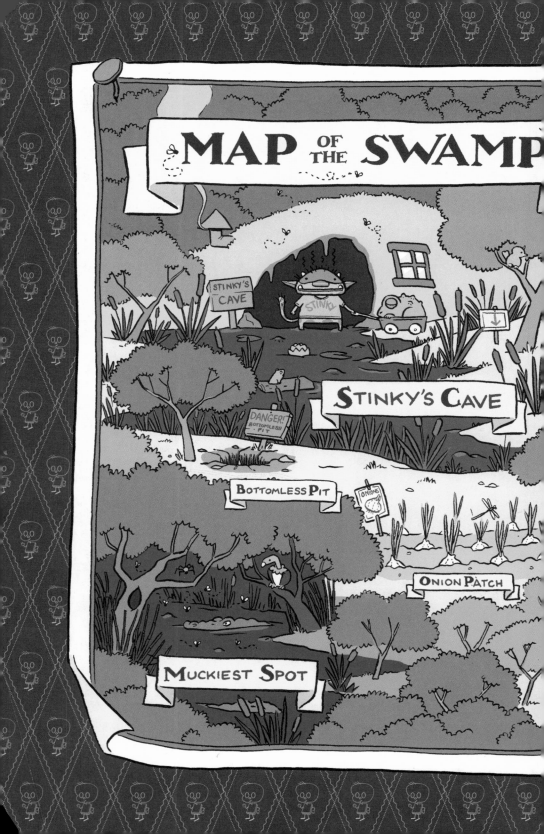

A THEODOR SEUSS GEISEL HONOR BOOK

A BOOKLIST NOTABLE CHILDREN'S BOOK

A BANK STREET COLLEGE OF EDUCATION BEST CHILDREN'S BOOK OF THE YEAR

Editorial Director: FRANÇOISE MOULY
Advisor: ART SPIEGELMAN

Book Design: FRANÇOISE MOULY & JONATHAN BENNETT

Copyright © 2008 RAW Junior, LLC, 27 Greene Street, New York, NY 10013. Printed in Singapore by Tien Wah Press (Pte.) Ltd. No part of this book may be used or reproduced in any manner whatsoever without written permission except in the case of brief quotations embodied in critical articles and reviews. All rights reserved. TOON Books, LITTLE LIT® and THE LITTLE LIT LIBRARY are trademarks of RAW Junior, LLC. Library of Congress Control Number: 2007943857

ISBN 13: 978-1-935179-03-0   ISBN 10: 1-935179-03-9
Paperback edition
10 9 8 7 6 5 4 3 2 1

CHAPTER ONE

7

9

Towns have *kids*...

...and kids don't like swamps. They like to take *baths!*

It makes me *so* mad!

GRR!

STINKY

GRR!

CHAPTER TWO

I'll go hide.

HEE! HEE!

Here he comes!

♪

≋SNIFF≋

HUH? What's that smell?

19

And so...

On to plan "B"!

BANG! BANG!

TOOLS

DAISY

Mmm... He needs that *hammer* to make his tree house.

Hammer

If I hide it, he'll go home!

20

28

30

Well, maybe **not** a **bottomless** pit! But it's **very** deep.

I'll **never** get out!

I'll **never** see my swamp again!!!

BONK!

BAW!

33

35

36

And then...

Ha! Wartbelly! I *missed* you!

CROAK!

Oh, I see! Daisy is *your* toad?

Yes! But I call her *Wartbelly*.

Let's call her **DAISY WARTBELLY!**

HA HA HA

CROAK!

Would you like an apple?

YUCK!

ER— I mean, thanks!

CHOMP!

38

ABOUT THE AUTHOR

ELEANOR DAVIS grew up in Tucson, Arizona. Instead of going out in the hot sun to play and make friends, she stayed alone in her room, drawing. She started working on *Stinky*, her first published book, while still a student at the Savannah College of Art and Design. *Stinky* earned her many honors including an Eisner Award nomination, and Eleanor was given the Russ Manning Promising Newcomer Award for it. Now Eleanor is widely praised as one of the coolest artists on the new comics scene.

She lives in Athens, Georgia, with her husband (who is also a cartoonist) and three cats (who are not).

Collect them all...
TOON BOOKS

JACK AND THE BOX
BY ART SPIEGELMAN

9×6, 32 PAGES
COLOR HARDCOVER
ISBN-13: 978-0-9799238-3-8
ISBN-10: 0-9799238-3-2

SILLY LILLY
AND THE FOUR SEASONS
BY AGNÈS ROSENSTIEHL

9×6, 36 PAGES
COLOR HARDCOVER
ISBN-13: 978-0-9799238-1-4
ISBN-10: 0-9799238-1-6

LITTLE MOUSE GETS READY
BY JEFF SMITH

9×6, 32 PAGES
COLOR HARDCOVER
ISBN-13: 978-1-935179-01-6
ISBN-10: 1-935179-01-2

BENNY AND PENNY
IN JUST PRETEND
BY GEOFFREY HAYES

6×9, 32 PAGES
COLOR HARDCOVER
ISBN-13: 978-0-9799238-0-7
ISBN-10: 0-9799238-0-8

BENNY AND PENNY
IN THE BIG NO-NO!
BY GEOFFREY HAYES

6×9, 32 PAGES
COLOR HARDCOVER
ISBN-13: 978-0-9799238-9-0
ISBN-10: 0-9799238-9-1

LUKE ON THE LOOSE
BY HARRY BLISS

6×9, 32 PAGES
COLOR HARDCOVER
ISBN-13: 978-1-935179-00-9
ISBN-10: 1-935179-00-4

STINKY
BY ELEANOR DAVIS

6×9, 40 PAGES
COLOR HARDCOVER
ISBN-13: 978-0-9799238-4-5
ISBN-10: 0-9799238-4-0

MO AND JO: FIGHTING
TOGETHER FOREVER
BY DEAN HASPIEL
AND JAY LYNCH

6×9, 40 PAGES
COLOR HARDCOVER
ISBN-13: 978-0-9799238-5-2
ISBN-10: 0-9799238-5-9

OTTO'S ORANGE DAY
BY FRANK CAMMUSO
AND JAY LYNCH

6×9, 40 PAGES
COLOR HARDCOVER
ISBN-13: 978-0-9799238-2-1
ISBN-10: 0-9799238-2-4

BRINGING NEW READERS TO THE PLEASURE OF COMICS!